Puns Upon a Rhyme

A Collection of Limericks to Tickle Your Fancy

Kevin Lucas

Puns Upon a Rhyme

A Collection of Limericks to Tickle Your Fancy

Kevin Lucas

Puns Upon a Rhyme

Kevin Lucas

ZIMBELL HOUSE PUBLISHING
UNION LAKE MICHIGAN

For permission requests, write to the publisher at the address below:
"Attention: Permissions Coordinator"
Zimbell House Publishing, LLC
PO Box 1172
Union Lake, Michigan 48387
mail to: info@zimbellhousepublishing.com

Published in the United States by Zimbell House Publishing
http://www.ZimbellHousePublishing.com
All Rights Reserved

© 2018 Kevin Lucas

Print ISBN: 978-1-947210-07-3
Kindle ISBN: 978-1-947210-08-0
Digital ISBN: 978-1-947210-09-7
Library of Congress Control Number: 2017917782

First Edition: January 2018
10 9 8 7 6 5 4 3 2 1

ZIMBELL HOUSE PUBLISHING
UNION LAKE

Dedication

To my daughter Lindsay, my greatest creation.

Acknowledgements

There are too many people to thank for the honed limericks you will read in these pages. I would, however, like to acknowledge four people who have helped immensely in this fine-tuning process—Chris J. Strolin, Janet McConnaughey, Joanna Keene, and Jesse Frankovich.

Thank you.

A Collection of
Limericks
to
Tickle Your
Fancy

Kevin Lucas

Sue walks by with a strut and a sway,
Prompting guys to cast eyeballs her way.
They can't help it; they're drawn
To that gal who's real gone.
And their girlfriends are left to cry, *"Hey!"*

I was critical, toeing the ledge
Between health and becoming a veg.
On TV? The election.
The final projection
Has pushed me right over the edge.

"That smell is horrendous." "Yes. Quite."
"You're to blame." "Absolutely. You're right.
That's a fact. No disputin'.
For certain. Darn tootin'.
Those beans have me tootin' all night."

"Your head's on the chopping block, Fred."
It's not just getting canned that I dread;
I so angered my boss
That I'm facing a loss
Execution style—"Off with his head!"

Post cardiac surgery, Kim
Expressed love to her doc on a whim.
Now she says with despair,
"Guess he just doesn't care,
And I opened my heart out to him!"

In football, a down is a chance
For the team with the ball to advance.
With ten yards, at least, gained,
The possession's retained.
If you get to the end zone, don't dance.

What an ass! Listen, don't get me started.
Profane, narcissistic, cold-hearted ...
So much more I could say,
But today's when we pay
Our respects to our dearly departed.

Power shovels dig sediment massed
In the waterways where it was cast.
This got me to thinkin',
That city that's Incan
And lost—can one dredge up the past?

If an item's exchanged, it's replaced
By a new one, like when I was faced
With your nagging nonstop.
I decided to swap
You for someone who's more to my taste.

An apostrophe?! Jeez! Shoulda known
Not to etch that. The epitaph shown
Is so wrong in its flagrance.
PICK A ROSE AND IT'S FRAGRANCE
REMAINS is, alas, carved in stone.

I've evolved on that point in all candor.
To say that I've flip-flopped is slander.
I've amended my view
Over time, just like you,
But in *your* case, you did it to pander.

I'm part of an atheist squad
Of performers. The concept is odd,
As revealed in the skit
Where we ponder a bit,
Entertaining the notion of God.

He's the flavor du jour, the in thing.
Very likely, he'll soon not be king
Of the mountain. His crowd,
Who is currently wowed,
Will move on. He'll be yesterday's fling.

"Kids, thanks for the card. Tell your mother
Today I go choreless." "Oh, brother!
I heard that! This one day
In June, the third Sunday,
For you is just like any other!"

"How is med school?" Neglecting to tell
My old man I dropped out, that things fell
By the wayside (I lack
Both the interest and knack),
I just smiled and replied, "Going well."

Jane's not plain anymore—no, she's not—
Since her makeover. Changing a lot,
She's a six, maybe, now;
But she's still not like "Wow!"
Let's be real. She's a far cry from hot.

Times were good, and I made lots of bread.
Love was true with the woman I wed.
So I thought. Times turned bad,
And I lost all I had,
And my fair-weather wife up and fled.

That class I signed up for? All told,
There was one other student enrolled.
With the failure to draw
Enough interest, we saw
Origami Enthusiasts fold.

You've gotten my dander up, son!
I'm so mad and annoyed, 'cause not one
Thing I've asked you to do
Since last weekend have you
Made the slightest attempt to get done!

"Are you challenging me?" Don asked Ron.
"I am so gonna beat you. Game on!"
So they battled it out,
Downing hot dogs and kraut.
Now the winner's last out of the john.

What's the temp of a body at ease?
Most would say, "37 degrees."
As a Yankee, I state,
"I prefer 98
.6 Fahrenheit. Celsius? *Please*."

"We don't need no" is not one negation,
But two; this creates cancellation.
Double negatives make
For a positive take.
Hey, Pink Floyd! So, we *need* education?

On a clean-living lifestyle, I pride myself.
By the teachings of Jesus, I guide myself.
But my ne'er-do-well twin,
Who's conjoined, lives in sin,
And I'm greatly distressed—I'm beside myself!

Patriotic personifications
Are seen in cartoonist creations.
Brother Jonathan (who?)
Would lose out to the new
Uncle Sam ("I Want You") illustrations.

'Cause of harsh puritanical views
Via blue laws, we're down with the blues.
I strongly object
To a Sabbath respect
That enforces a ban on all booze.

Chuck Cunningham syndrome is when,
As if writ with erasable pen,
The scripts of a show
Let a character go,
And he's never referred to again.

The hijackers took full control
With the Capitol Building their goal;
But the passengers learned
Of the towers that burned
And would execute bravely—"Let's roll!"

"You used to get picked on? By who?"
"By a mean kid in school that I knew.
Then one day after class,
I just whomped on his ass."
"That's impressive! Well, bully for you!"

"We decided to go for a bite.
Gee, that man is a talker, all right,"
Said Evander of Mike.
"This I didn't much like.
He was chewing my ear off all night."

From one action, results are direct
In the domino (ripple) effect.
Though each change may be small,
Set in motion are all
The events that will interconnect.

Your extravagant plans? Unfulfilled,
A result of the castles you build
In the air. I've much doubt
That you'll carry them out.
But I *will* say at daydreams you're skilled.

When I used to come home to my wife
And her cooking, disasters were rife.
Now she orders Chinese
And, with cabbage to please,
She is bringing bok choy to my life.

See this cross-staff I bear? It's no chore
As I carry it proudly before
The archbishop. The prelate
Likes joking, "They sell it
On down at the crociary store."

Pre-potty, my daughter's a dancer.
I hurry to de-underpants her
And rush to the lav.
Soon she'll know, when you have
Calls of nature, it's best you should answer.

My friend said, "I'm fleet on my feet
When encountering gals who've been beat
With an ugly stick." "But,"
I informed him, "know what?
I'm sure looking at you is no treat."

My love life with Kelvin I'd cheer; oh,
His energy made him my hero.
Now his movement is nil.
He's so cold, lying still,
Making Kelvin an absolute zero.

"Where I'll relegate you is no mystery!"
Screamed Barb with rebuke that was blistery.
Her ex-beau was apprised
He'd be marginalized
And consigned to the ash heap of history.

"That degreed education of yours,"
Said my father, "will open most doors.
Opportunity knocks.
You won't find many locks."
"Dad, hold on. Not through mopping these floors."

I'm not used to my mirrored reflection.
My past has no trace of connection.
The new me is disguised.
My whole life was revised
Upon entering Witness Protection.

Imagine the trunk of a tree
With two branches; my brother and me
Are dicephalus twins—
At the neck he begins.
I'm a bum. Oddly, he's an M.D.

Any hope that I might have had flew
Out the window when tryouts were through.
The director said, "No.
Not the type. You can go.
Oh, and please don't call us, we'll call you."

Contradiction in terms—an expression
Or phrase (e.g., *passive aggression*)
That's false necessarily
(*Trusting you warily;*
Ethical legal profession).

On the chain gang, my sorrows were rife.
I broke free with the help of my wife.
Now I'm kept from the joys
Of nights out with the boys.
Take this new ball and chain. Give me life!

"When the world ends," said God, "I'll be checkin'
Who's evil, who's not, and will beckon
The good souls to save.
Judgment Day will be grave
For the rest. Call it doomsday; I reckon."

Our connubial rites will take place
On June 4, when we stand face to face
And we say our *I do's*.
Should she choose to refuse,
You're my backup, my love, just in case.

It seems God up above, the Great Giver
Of Blessings, gives nary a sliver
To me. All my prayers
Are ignored, like "Who cares?"
So I ask Him, "What *am* I, chopped liver?"

Nag, nag, nag! I can't bear it and grin. It
Decreases my life span each minute.
Best get out while I can.
If I stay, this young man
Better plan for a grave; I'll be in it.

"Disencharm me, oh Wizard! You granted
My wish with a spell that you planted.
Now the babes that I draw
Talk and talk—major flaw.
Set me free!" I became disenchanted.

Her personal phone calls at work
Never ended; they drove me berserk.
In a frenzy of violence,
I killed her. The silence
From motionless lips is a perk.

The blueskins—their skin wasn't blue—
Held a strict puritanical view.
Presbyterians, grave
In the way they'd behave,
Were a solemn bunch. Fun was taboo.

"Gonna come to my school graduation?"
Asked Jethro in heightened elation.
"I passed the sixth grade.
I will sure have it made!
I done got me a edumacation!"

"Your deterioration is slow.
Will this lead to your death? Likely so.
It's called circling the drain."
"Doc, no need to explain,
'Cept for this--Is it clockwise I'll go?"

The reruns I've watched since the eighties.
Three girls and their mom, lovely ladies,
Team up with a man
With three boys. This big clan
And their maid was a bunch called the Bradys.

With my friend, I agreed to compete
In a race, although neither got beat.
When we finished our run
In the hot desert sun,
We were both number one—a dead heat.

Grampa smiled an edentulous grin
For a photo with all of us kin.
Gramma turned with a sneer
And a scold all could hear—
"You old fool! Put your dentures back in!"

Facing Louis was no day at camp.
The Brown Bomber was heavyweight champ.
Joe's punches had sting.
He was king of the ring,
And he later appeared on a stamp.

Thumbs down? But on what is that based?"
The restaurant critic I faced
Offered no explanation,
No justification.
There's just no accounting for taste.

The water rose up from the mean sea
And washed out that spider so teensy.
Our eight-legged friend,
We assume, met its end.
What's the chance it survived? Eensy-weensy.

Bread and circuses work very well
To keep citizens under the spell
Of their leaders. Contentment
Replaces resentment.
Less likely they'll want to rebel.

Though they share the same room, kids today
Say no words; still, they're chatting away
With their hand-held machines.
Instant messaging means
They compunicate. Speaking's passé.

Thus far, I'd no dating success.
As yet, I have failed to impress.
Up till now, I'd no clue
Why chicks feel as they do.
Then I looked in the mirror—"Ah, yes."

Nancy Noone second-naturedly natters.
"Blah, blah, blah," she incessantly chatters.
Her friends pray for strength
As she babbles at length
About mind-numbing, trivial matters.

"Your relationship's losing its fizz?"
Asked my mom, a buttinsky. It is,
But she constantly peddles
Advice as she meddles.
I told her, "Mom, none of your biz."

"I converted the code to plain text,"
A decipherer said. "Now what's next
Are the much tougher reads
Of the wants and the needs
Of a woman—that's got me perplexed."

Though our differing views we hold strong,
It's important we all get along.
Disagreements we have
Can be soothed with a salve
Of calm words. Still, the fact is you're wrong.

"I pine for a hookup with Beth."
"Kev, keep dreaming. More likely, your death
Will come first, so don't wait
For some dubious date.
She's not into you. Don't hold your breath."

"That gospel song's great! How I revel
In God's holy word!" exclaimed Neville.
Then he heard the song played
In reverse, and it made
Him repulsed; it says, "Worship the Devil."

Bittersweetly, my pleasure was met
With a tinge of both pain and regret.
With the good came the bad.
I felt happy and sad
When I won playing Russian roulette.

My pre-arranged husband's Todd Rodham.
My parents asked, "Know where we got him?"
He's the dregs and a sap,
Lazy ass piece of crap.
"Let me guess. From a barrel, the bottom."

Sister Rose leads a life black and white.
Diverse interests she has when it's light.
When the moon's out, the same
Beastly rut is her game;
She's a creature of habit by night.

Since that shipment came in, we're in tears
Here at Madame Tussauds. It appears
We've an oversupply—
I mean WAY over. Why,
We have wax coming out of our ears!

My boomerang kid had a knack
Of returning, 'cause money he'd lack
To pay bills. Now I'm thrilled;
Early curfew has killed
Any chance that he'll find his way back.

Milk is best if it's used by the date
On the carton. This morning at 8,
I went down for a cup,
But I nearly threw up.
Seems I made me some cafe au late.

Milton Berle said, "That joke that I told?
Punch it up with some chuckles of old."
So the soundman came through
With canned laughter on cue.
"See? I told you that joke was pure gold."

"You asked for the moon? You're insane!"
"Maybe so. Still it worked to my gain.
My six-figure demand
Was dismissed out of hand,
So I left ... on the company plane."

Lincoln, Washington, Jackson, and Grant
Are dead presidents. Two others can't
Claim to ever have led
The U.S., 'cause they're dead;
But deny them cash portraits? We shan't.

A movie they put on the shelf
Stars Hugh Beaumont, who's playing an elf.
Tony Dow has a role;
He's a miner of coal.
Jerry Mathers appears as himself.

The caterers came with much food,
And a very fine banquet ensued
When the host said, "Dig in!"
I know gluttony's a sin,
But I just didn't want to be rude.

I'm a kook, nearly all will agree.
But my past is my benchmark, you see,
And I'm always this strange.
Thus, there hasn't been change
From my baseline. Weird's normal for me.

Said urology patient, Max Hubble,
"My pee stream is coming out double.
One hits the bowl fine,
But the stray makes a line
For the floor." Said the doc, "Urine trouble."

Though my dog's life, unpleasant and wretched,
Was stressing me out for a stretch, it,
Thank God, turned around.
There is joy to be found.
All it takes is for one to go fetch it.

Said my screener, "A guy on line three
Claims he's God." So I took it to see.
Boomed a voice loud and clear,
"Your time's done on this sphere!
Son, I'm calling you home! Come with me!"

"The irregular shape of this spot
Means it's blotchily made, does it not?"
"Ooh-ooh-ooooh!" "Mr. Horshack?"
"That ink stain by Rorschach
Looks just like a birthmark I got."

I'm in stunned disbelief. Am I seeing
An extraterrestrial being?
It's right by those trees.
"Earthling, privacy, please.
Do you mind? Can't you see that I'm peeing?"

I was told by the store clerk, "It's clear
You've not reached yet your twenty-first year.
You're not drinking age." *Sigh!*
Guys, the closest supply
I could buy for the kegger's near beer.

The Last Supper accounts exclude Fred.
This forgotten apostle broke bread
With the rest, but his toast,
A bad pun—"To our host!
Get it? Host?"—made them mad, so he fled.

"Honey, how do I look in this dress?"
"I could care less." "You *couldn't* care less.
Unconcerned to the max,
With an interest quite lax,
You don't give a damn." "Sorry, but yes."

"That charades-obsessed guy's gonna throw
A big party tonight. Wanna go?"
"What? That pantomime geek,
Who just acts and won't speak,
And we guess words and phrases? Uh, no."

Yelled the patron, "My soup has a fly!"
In surprise came my echoed reply
In a question. "Your soup
Has a fly? Here's a scoop.
Care to try, on the house, shoo-fly pie?"

One night, I was having a swig,
When the cops came to raid our blind pig,
Where the alcohol sale
Was illegal. The scale
Of the riot that followed was big.

Oh, you great comprehensor, you've come
To full knowledge; you've mastered the sum.
That includes what you know
About me. If you go
To my folks' and I'm mentioned, play dumb.

I'm bequeathing a corneal prize
To an eye bank upon my demise.
Then a surgeon can make
One with vision opaque
Come to look at the world through my eyes.

My discipline's history, class.
That's my branch of instruction. You'll pass
If you do all the work.
If the work, though, you shirk,
You'll be history—out on your ass.

The girl who first won my affection,
My first love, didn't make a connection
With me, not one tad.
I was grateful and glad
If she looked in my general direction.

I met Anne in the clubhouse one day.
She resembles a cow. I asked, "Hey,
What's your board game of choice?"
Thinking best not to voice—
"Cowy Anne, what's your game? Can I play?"

Biosocially, forces combine.
They're behind this affliction of mine.
DNA made me fat,
Though it doesn't help that
It's on junk food I'm most apt to dine.

The flames from the arsons were hearty
Last Halloween eve. My friend Artie
Fell victim to one
Whose sick notion of fun
Is a Devil's Night house warming party.

To my first wife came bodily harm,
And my second, alas, bought the farm.
Will my luck turn around?
There's a pen pal I found
From my cell. Maybe third time's a charm.

"I'm eating for two!" exclaimed Sue,
Who, in just a few weeks, will be due.
Cried the waiter, "That's great!"
He then turned to her mate
And, in jest, asked the porker, "You too?"

"I was feeling left out," said McGuinn.
"All my buddies from high school had been
In the army, and so
When we meet now, I go
Wearing camo—I want to blend in."

You dwell on your failures and pout.
Then it falls on deaf ears when I shout
All the time not to beat
Yourself up. I'll repeat
It no longer, so knock yourself out.

Most everyone knows you don't dare a bull.
In a similar vein, it's a terrible
Resolve you incite
If you're picking a fight
With one dormant whose might is unbearable.

The cosmos, when reaching the max
In its size from expansion, contracts.
Gravitational force
Makes all matter switch course
And implode. Down the road though. Relax.

This inventor, known hither and yon
As the greatest, would happen upon
An idea. That's when
Thomas Edison then
Had an overhead light bulb go on.

Dumb and silent we'll be if we're bled
Of our speech freedom, Washington said.
If absence of voice
Is the dictator's choice,
Then, like sheep to the slaughter, we're led.

"Per their dress code, they couldn't refuse
Giving service, Your Honor." "You lose.
Something else they had meant
By that sign. When you went,
You wore *only* a shirt and some shoes."

Fine matter collects to embrace
And form clouds; they're all over the place
On a much higher sphere.
Cosmic dust we have here,
So it's good there's a vacuum in space.

Early on, shortly after the start
Of my social awareness, my heart
Ruled the way I perceived.
Over time, I achieved
Intellectual sway. Now I'm smart.

With no jobs in my field, it was wise
That this graduate thought to devise
A contingency plan.
I'm a practical man,
Not too proud. "So, with that, you want fries?"

A parachute jumper he's not.
In this movie, no airplane you'll spot.
There's no free-falling guy
Dropping out of the sky.
That's a chutist. *This* shootist gets shot.

With my terminal illness a cage,
I am soon to break free. The last page
In the journey of life
Has been reached. With my wife
And kids bedside, I exit the stage.

"At airports, what's not an okay word
Is *checked*," I informed my kid Hayward.
"Your bag should go in
A plane's overhead bin.
Son, a carry-on doesn't go wayward."

A conclave, in secretive cloak,
Meets to choose from its ranks the one bloke
Who will change his profession
To pope. From this session,
Their choice always goes up in smoke.

If you step out of line, they're the ones
Who will rap on your knuckles or buns.
They're a very feared force.
I am speaking, of course,
Of the disciplinarian nuns.

"In my *other* job, I'm a recorder
Of things as they happened; a sorter
Of facts from the past
From the first to the last,"
Said the waitress who wrote down my order.

An ex-hippie I know likes to cling,
And she'll constantly phone. So, last spring
I got caller ID.
If the name that I see
Shows as "Freedom," I just let it ring.

From the dead letter office, there came
Sacks of mail with the "Santa Claus" name.
Said the judge, "Case dismissed,
Since the feds all insist
That Kris Kringle and he are the same."

It's in fantasyland you reside.
You imagine that gal by your side.
Sorry, bud. In your dreams.
She won't go to extremes
And date dorks. She's too cool for that ride.

In our junior high musical, Deb'll
Play opposite Rob, who's a rebel.
His disdain for convention
Gets women's attention.
That bad boy ain't nothing but treble.

As June Cleaver, she'll always remain
In our hearts in a motherly vein.
Barbara Billingsley then
Spoofed that character when,
In a film, she spoke jive on a plane.

Said my dad, with the help of a graph,
"What you earn in this 'job' won't be half
Of a *real* job. The thrills
Of a club won't pay bills.
A comedian? Don't make me laugh."

Pilot Jones was one helluva guy!
God has taken his soul to the sky.
At the funeral Mass,
Flight attendants now pass
By his casket and tell him, "Buh bye."

Human apathy's much more routine
The more people there are on the scene
Of a victim's distress.
Chance of aid is much less.
We think, "Let someone else intervene."

The PI that I hired to hover
In secret, in hopes to discover
If someone had part
Of my wife's suspect heart,
Is the guy I found out is her lover.

Incognito's the look Judy tries
When her former beau Rudy she spies.
Does that gal think she's kiddin'?
Her looks can't be hidden
With glasses her only disguise.

The result of a hookup gone bad,
My daughter's best friend never had
Any male in the role
Of a father. That hole
Has been filled; I'm her surrogate dad.

My brother's a pest. Shoulda slugged
The dumb schmuck when he constantly tugged
On my arm, asking, "Bro,
Where'd my book of maps go?"
But, not seeing his atlas, I shrugged.

I was given a glowing review.
Complimentary comments I drew.
I'm so grateful and glad
That my boss is my dad
And a very good bull-shitter too.

As a surgeon, my doctor's a jewel,
But his follow-up conduct is cruel.
My concerns he attacks.
Bedside manner he lacks.
They don't teach that in medical school.

Actors' bodies of work have some stinkers.
Career-wise, they're not often sinkers.
If enough, though, get made
Of the D or F grade,
Stars may pray, "Better scripts!" Wishful thinkers.

"I've been dealt a bad hand, God. I'm fat,
I'm not smart, and I'm one ugly cat."
"Lose some weight. Read more books.
In regards to your looks,
Listen, Kevin. I'm sorry 'bout that."

Violinists use bows when they play,
And these bows are called fiddlesticks. They,
For some reason, became
What some people exclaim
When they're mad and they watch what they say.

To an auction I went and laid eyes
On what would have been best of all buys.
Other men expressed like,
But the man at the mike
Said, "My wife isn't biddable, guys."

That plain model who posed for my etching?
To say that she's cute would be stretching
Credulity, yet
What I want she will get
And bring back to me. Boy, is she fetching!

My sanity's near on the skids,
Doing this, doing that for my kids.
I so need some alone time,
Some me time, my own time,
Which parenthood often forbids.

Our Southern politeness is part
Of our charm. If you're not very smart,
Not a brain in your head,
And if something you said
Is just dumb, we'll exclaim, "Bless your heart!"

God, my prayer's still unanswered. My yen
Is to date gals who rate a strong ten.
Let it be. Make it so.
Work your magic. Hello?
Are you there? Can I get an amen?

The Establishment keeps a position
Of power by name recognition.
They're the permanent class.
Real reform gets a pass,
And the kicking of cans is tradition.

Constant carping on trivial flaws
Led to reaching the last of my straws.
In death, she now pays
For her fault-finding ways,
And the court system found I'd just cause.

"Men, I'm hoping to see a clean fight,"
Said the bout's referee. Since that night,
There's been one rules addition.
The boxing commission
Amended them slightly—*Don't bite.*

He was thawed from sub-zero degrees.
"Mr. Powers, evacuate please."
Two, three minutes pass by
For this bladder-full guy,
But completion's not reached. Still he pees.

Circa '71 in Big Sur,
Maybe '72 ... I'm not sure,
On a commune we met,
But that time I forget.
I regret that whole decade's a blur.

"Jeans and T-shirt? To see that is brutal,"
Said stylishly dressed Yankee Doodle,
A dandy, "but passion
For clothing of fashion
Is what I'd call using your noodle."

"Do you say Michiganian?" "No.
I prefer Michigander. Although
Lincoln coined it to diss
Our state's governor, this
Is the term by which most of us go."

If men shave in the morning, by late
Afternoon some slight stubble's their fate.
They've a shadow at five,
And it could well deprive
Them of winning a TV debate.

Master Satan is calling on you.
You're his favorite barber—it's true—
'Cause you're keenly aware
How he wishes his hair
To be styled. Give the Devil his do.

"Have you fixed on a date for the wedding?"
"Yes. We've chosen the time and the setting,
The month and the day,
But I really can't say
If it's Jenny or Joanie I'm getting."

A blue-tail fly bit Massa's thigh.
Then his horse took off, bucking the guy
From the saddle. He fell
In a ditch, and—oh, well—
I don't care. (He was left there to die.)

I wore Burger King's Flame—once a spray
With a flame-broiled burger bouquet.
When I asked a girl out,
That cologne made her shout,
"No! You stink!" I groused, "Have it *your* way."

Medieval tribes Lucas and Lawson
Fought feudally. Neither will toss in
The towel just yet.
Hell, these clans even met
On TV with the host Richard Dawson.

"I'll deal now with this matter," said Keith,
"Or the problems that stir underneath
Will see light. Then the sum
Of my troubles will come
Back to bite me with much bigger teeth."

She gave me the buzzer effect,
Saying, "Surely, you didn't expect
I'd say yes." I said, "So,
Then I guess that's a no?"
She yelled, "Ding, ding, ding, ding! You're correct!"

When a Hamilton slur made the news,
The VP, Aaron Burr, blew a fuse
And demanded retraction.
None came. Duel action
Ensued, which saw Hamilton lose.

My mom's just thrown one thing away
Of my dad's, who passed on back in May.
Eighty-sixing his stuff
Has proved terribly tough,
But she *did* toss his silk negligée.

When he stepped in his tub, water rose
With its volume displaced. I suppose
Archimedes flipped out,
With "Eureka!" his shout,
As he ran through the streets with no clothes.

At corporate, they finally got smart.
The execs of this grocery mart
Allow scooters for just
The disabled. You must,
If you're lazy or fat, push a cart.

Whatever your traveling mode
Via Italy's streets, my map showed
That it's true what they say.
An approachable way
To reach Rome is to take any road.

First, they came for (arrested, detained)
All the Socialists. No one complained.
We weren't them. Then their troops
Kept on rounding up groups.
My turn came, but no voices remained.

I dated my patient. No more.
Our relationship's health was quite poor.
With our history rough
And no physical stuff,
I thought, "What am I seeing her for?"

I was taught how to spot a good deal
By my mom, but I totally feel,
With small items, that I've
Got a better way—five-
Finger discounts. They're grabbed for a steal.

"Take a shower, my daughter," I said,
"Cuz we're going to Grandma's." Ahead
Of her shower, her aim
Was to finish the game
On her phone. She said, "Wait till I'm dead."

"Fee-fi-fo-fum!" came the yell
Of the giant, who sensed a bad smell
From the Englishman Jack.
He continued, "*Ack! Ack!
You filled up on those beans! Bloody hell!"*

With the end of December upon
All the world, Father Time marches on
To the sunset. Before
Time goes out the back door,
Baby New Year's been passed the baton.

A terrorist yelled among peers
At a party, "Let's lift up our beers!
Here's a toast to our health,
To our wealth, and our stealth!
Oh, yeah. Death to America! Cheers!"

Though born to the purple (noblesse
Is my birthright), I have to confess
That this prince would bring shame
To the family name
Were it known I like wearing a dress.

Richard's fettered. He writes from Fort Lee,
"I'm in shackles. Please help. Set me free."
That reminds me—I'm bound
By a cheese block I downed.
Now I can't get this poop outta me!

Easter Sunday my mom blew a gasket.
"You're not going to church?!" Why'd she ask it?
I'm a heathen. She knows.
Eggs and candy I chose.
"You are going to hell in that basket!"

Echo chambers on Facebook are all
That she seeks when she writes on her wall
About matters political.
I was too often critical,
Which led to her friendship withdrawal.

Parabolically arcing across
Were the chainsaws I happened to toss.
What I'd planned was they'd land
In the opposite hand,
But I suffered a permanent loss.

"See this stone, small and flat? See me grip it
With a curled index finger then whip it
'Cross the lake. See it bounce
In increasing amounts.
Wanna play ducks and drakes?" "Meh, let's skip it."

My magical world was unmatched.
It was beautiful. Then they dispatched
Me away to be taught
Analytical thought.
Now I'm clinical—coldly detached.

My comatose kid brother, Seth,
Has a will, saying, "Should I draw breath
With machines to support
Just my shell, please abort.
Give me liberty. Give me my death."

The carousel kept going round,
But my baggage was not to be found
When I got to L.A.
I learned later that day
That my luggage was Washington-bound.

At this radio station, I'm zappin'
The four-letter words people happen
To say on the air.
That's my dump button there.
I'll be *bleep*, in deep *bleep* if caught nappin'.

A faux accent I do of a Brit
To impress my hot gal. I admit
It was fun at the start
When this ruse won her heart.
Now she's hinting at marriage. Oh, shit!

She assigned a team project. It irks
When you find you're the sole one who works.
For this A you all see
You can thank only me—
A committee of one. Stupid jerks!

Beyond help, you seem largely content
With your many neuroses. Hell-bent
On repairing your head
Was your shrink, but instead,
In that aim, he made nary a dent.

The contract I signed on the line
Contained overlooked print that was fine.
Said the Devil who hid
In the details, "Hey kid,
Enjoy fame, but your soul is now mine."

Diverse demographics she seeks.
Many focus groups help with the tweaks
Of her message. She learns
Of their cares and concerns,
And then, armed with this feedback, she speaks.

With her gaze on his flesh, Ann began
Her dishonest and secretive plan
As she selfishly drew
Him away. That tattoo
Artist tramp had designs on my man.

My twin daughters are gay. Is it fate?
Would conversion make gayness abate?
Though it worked (they denied
Who they were deep inside),
They reverted. I can't keep 'em straight.

"GOD IS DEAD" some graffiti insisted.
"Whoever believes that is twisted,"
Said a theist, "for sure."
I, a skeptic, concur.
God can't die if He never existed.

For the sake of this joke, let's assume
Jesus Christ, when He dressed in His room,
Put on drawers. You might find
This amusing. What kind
Did He wear? Answer—Fruit of Thy Womb.

I died in a bathtub one night
At an inn. When the guests there catch sight
Of my ghost, they're less scared
By my presence compared
To my birthday suit causing a fright.

Coulrophobia, most experts say,
Isn't recognized. Please put away
All your fears of my nose,
My huge feet, and wild clothes,
'Cause this clown needs some lovin'. *Hey! Hey!*

The scene was surreal: coffin shut,
Dad inside. He then opened it. *What
In God's name???* We turned white
At the burial site.
Then the funeral director yelled, "Cut!"

Said a prudish tattoo artist, "Fine.
I can give you a tramp stamp design,
But I'm putting restrictions
On lower depictions.
Your butt's where I'm drawing the line."

Marvin Gaye was a singer of note,
Who had many a hit; some he wrote.
He was part of the stable
Of Motown, a label.
Sweet soulfulness flowed from his throat.

Since I finished this ark, God expects
Me to round up and fill this ship's decks
With all beasts two by two,
Male and female. No clue
How I'm s'posed to, on some, check the sex.

With brain farts, we mentally lapse,
Temporarily suffering gaps
In our thinking. We're caught
Having lost trains of thought
As, abruptly, our neurons take naps.

"Dummy up. With no knowledge revealed
To the cops, it might act as a shield
To my capture." "Hey chap,"
Said the guy on my lap,
"This might help—keep your *own* two lips sealed."

"You are just like your mother. A lot."
"Don't you *ever* say that. No, I'm not!"
"It's a compliment, hon.
Can't I praise my wife, one
Who's so clear-off-the-chart, smokin' hot?"

No refrigerant? That's a disgrace!
For this play, we need fog. Go and chase
Down some packets, a few
Solid-form CO$_2$,
Or there'll be no dry ice in the place.

A woman with child cried, "Hey rummy!"
To a drunk who was getting too chummy.
"We're not friends. I don't know
Who you are, in fact, so
Get your scuzzy, damn hand off my tummy!"

"That's one frickin' huge layer cake! Jeez!
Someone get me a big-ass knife, please,"
Said a guest at a party.
"Just what," asked some smartie,
"Is an ass knife? Does that cut the cheese?"

On the court are my wife and a freak.
At this moment, right now, as we speak,
They're delaying the game.
I cry, "Ethel, for shame!
Get your clothes on, you hussy! Don't streak!"

"You're uncultured and awkward." "What of it?"
"You lack social graces." "You love it."
"You're ill-mannered, ill-bred ..."
"Was it something I said?"
"You're so terribly gauche." "Oh, go shove it!"

"Hey, it's Bjorn, right? You used to not pay
Any heed to religion." "Today,
I make calls door to door,
House to house, in God's corps."
"Bjorn, no way! A Jehovah?" "Ya, way."

Last Friday, I ceased to exist
And was met by St. Pete, who dismissed
My poor soul, saying, "Kevin,
You're three steps from Heaven,
But sorry, you're not on the list."

This tale would surprise even Ripley.
Two singers named Brewer and Shipley
Got banned with "One Toke"
While two Welk folks, no joke,
Sang this "spiritual" wholly unhiply.

"My whole family is gonna be there,"
Said a lady, near death, in a chair.
"So before my life's done,
I am making just one
Dying wish. Will you color my hair?"

Certain shows that were favorites of mine
From the past, I will binge-watch online.
From episode one
Through each season, I run,
To the last, where I note the decline.

Easter Sunday at church, said the priest,
"Jesus Christ is the bread of life. Feast
On the Lord as we pray.
He is risen today."
My first thought, "Is His Father the yeast?"

Norma Jean, in the sordid affair,
Became fragile and weak in despair.
It was too much to handle.
They found this young candle
In the wind with her frailty laid bare.

She eats like a bird on a date.
Very little she picks off her plate.
With her doggy-bagged meal
At date's end, she can feel
Her true self; scarfing down just can't wait.

Once at home, she then eats like a horse.
She's relieved to give in to the force
Of her hunger alone
With no censuring tone
About all that she eats in one course.

A new mother said, "There's been a gap in
My memory. What made this happen?
Getting pregnant. I think
There's a definite link,
And right now, I'm just thinkin' of nappin'."

"Though your deathbed conversion was swell,
There's a notion I want to dispel.
Your awareness is great,
But you can't come this late
To the party," said God. "Go to Hell."

I was born in a hurricane, son.
The most difficult work I get done.
I can handle extreme
Situations full steam.
But your mom's PMS? That I shun.

Mom, the money you saved up for Fiji
Is gone. Daddy bet on a gee-gee
That lost at the track,
But he'll earn it all back.
He's downtown at red lights with a squeegee.

When faced with that challenge, you ran.
When life throws you curveballs, your plan
Should be tackling these things
With the courage of kings.
Have some balls! C'mon, Ann! Be a man!

Your psyche is still on the blink!
For crying out loud! Do you think
You could give me a break
With your issues? Chrissake!
You'll be driving this *shrink* to a shrink!

My rabbinical mentor said, "What it
Demands is dexterity." But it
Turned out that the blood
Made me faint. I went thud.
As a mohel, I couldn't quite cut it.

Official team records exclude
Exhibition games. One that I viewed
While in Athens last May,
Had participants play
In a throwback game—totally nude.

Your opinion I didn't solicit.
Express what you feel? I'll dismiss it.
Continue to add
Your two cents? I'll be glad
To just show you my ass and say, "Kiss it."

They didn't heed God's admonition—
Original sin, the commission
By Adam and Eve.
As expected, their leave
From the Garden had come to fruition.

There's a person I'm trying to seek
In myself, one who's better, whose cheek
Would be turned, who would do
Just as Jesus. But you
Make the prospect of that pretty bleak.

In all of these photos, my honey
Is gesturing ears of a bunny
Behind me. This prank
Is so old. Let's be frank—
Long ago it had ceased being funny.

My mom thought the time apropos,
With me preadolescent, to go
Have the talk. She said, "These
Are the facts of life ..." "*Please,*"
I chimed in, "death and taxes! I know!"

Over time, multitudinous sperm,
A gazillion, have set out to squirm
Because that's what they do.
Just a relative few
Have pierced ova and made it to term.

At Career Day, a cobbler named Paul
Said, "This instrument, pointed and small,
Is the tool that I use
To make holes in the shoes,
Which I stitch, pushing thread, and that's awl."

"Having mats under glasses is key
To protecting a surface, you see,"
Said a coaster while chatting
With bar patrons, adding,
"Hey everyone, drinks are on me!"

One blink, a brief instant in time,
Saw me pull on a trigger. Now I'm
Serving life. Was it worth
Taking one from this earth?
Yes. He really annoyed me, that mime.

I'm not gullible, Mom. For Pete's sake!
Boy and girl parts? Together they make
Human life? That tale's tall.
Look, I didn't just fall
Off the turnip truck. Gimme a break!

Big Tony had finished the carol
Then pointed at me his gun's barrel.
I'd cheerfully said
To the Mafia head,
"Don, I *love* your gay Christmas apparel!"

Success through hard work was his aim.
My old man really carved out a name
For himself. He took pride
Even more as a guide
For us children in doing the same.

Lois Lane scoffed, "Oh, *please!*" with derision
When told, by the boss, his decision.
"This next story takes two.
One reporter is you.
You'll be under Clark Kent's supervision."

Steven Wright Joke

Disfurnishment came in the night.
I was out, and a thief was on site.
He stole all I owned,
But he quickly atoned
And refurnished my dwelling just right

Assisted Reproductive Technology

We thought we would name our boy Art,
Since a lab in San Fran was his start.
(Sperm and eggs were combined.)
But his birth changed our mind.
He was born on the train; his name's Bart.

H.L. Mencken on Wisdom

Collectively, wisdom's a joke
If the masses are ignorant folk.
Just how much do they know?
If you bet, guessing low
Would ensure that you'd never go broke.

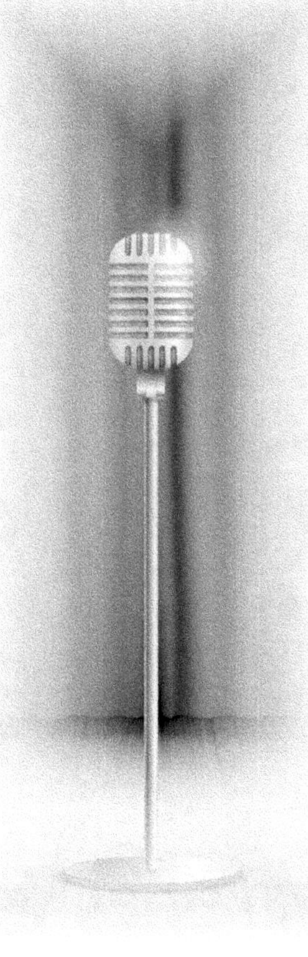

Kevin Lucas is the author of *Beats to the Punch: A Collection of Limericks* (available on Amazon). His interest in words and light verse rhyming poetry began at a young age.

Among his interests growing up were playing Scrabble, constructing crossword puzzles for his family, and writing song poems.

He has been writing limericks in earnest since 2006 and, to date, has composed over 3,000 limericks.

Other Works by Kevin Lucas

Beats to the Punch
The Little Blue Book of Limericks

A Note from the Publisher

Dear Reader,

Thank you for reading Kevin Lucas' collection, *Puns Upon a Rhyme.* We feel the best way to show appreciation for an author is by leaving a review. You may do so on any of the following sites:
www.ZimbellHousePublishing.com
Goodreads.com
Amazon.com
or Kindle.com

Join our mailing list to receive updates on new releases, discounts, bonus content, and other great books from Kevin Lucas and

Or visit us online to sign up at:

http://www.ZimbellHousePublishing.com